MW01136539

INSIDE COLLEGE
FOOTBALL

OHIO STATE
BUCKEYES

BY TONY HUNTER

SportsZone

An Imprint of Abdo Publishing
abdobooks.com

abdobooks.com

Published by Abdo Publishing, a division of ABDO, PO Box 398166, Minneapolis, Minnesota 55439. Copyright © 2021 by Abdo Consulting Group, Inc. International copyrights reserved in all countries. No part of this book may be reproduced in any form without written permission from the publisher. SportsZone™ is a trademark and logo of Abdo Publishing.

Printed in the United States of America, North Mankato, Minnesota
032020
092020

THIS BOOK CONTAINS
RECYCLED MATERIALS

Cover Photo: George Kubas II/AP Images
Interior Photos: Gene J. Puskar/AP Images, 5; Stephen Lew/Cal Sport Media/AP Images, 7; Ric Tapia/AP Images, 8; Courtesy of the Ohio History Connection, 11; Bettmann/Getty Images, 13, 15, 16, 43; AP Images, 19, 24, 26–27, 29; Harold Valentine/AP Images, 20; NFL/AP Images, 23; Paul Spinelli/AP Images, 32; Paul Sakuma/AP Images, 35; Ted S. Warren/AP Images, 37; Kiichiro Sato/AP Images, 38; Rick Scuteri/AP Images, 40

Editor: Patrick Donnelly
Series Designer: Nikki Nordby

Library of Congress Control Number: 2019954426

Publisher's Cataloging-in-Publication Data

Names: Hunter, Tony, author.
Title: Ohio State Buckeyes / by Tony Hunter
Description: Minneapolis, Minnesota : Abdo Publishing, 2021 | Series: Inside college
    football | Includes online resources and index.
Identifiers: ISBN 9781532192470 (lib. bdg.) | ISBN 9781644944691 (pbk.) | ISBN
    9781098210373 (ebook)
Subjects: LCSH: Ohio State Buckeyes (Football team)--Juvenile literature. | Universities
    and colleges--Athletics--Juvenile literature. | American football--Juvenile literature.
    | College sports--United States--History--Juvenile literature.
Classification: DDC 796.33263--dc23

TABLE OF
CONTENTS

CHAPTER 1

DOWNING
THE DUCKS

The Ohio State Buckeyes came into the 2014 season with national championship dreams. They were ranked fifth in the country and were loaded with talent. But the dream quickly turned into a nightmare. The Buckeyes lost their second game of the year at home to unranked Virginia Tech.

The upset stunned the 107,000 fans at Ohio Stadium and millions more around the country. Third-year head coach Urban Meyer was angry, too. But he also reminded his team there was plenty left to accomplish. To achieve their dreams, they had to settle for nothing less than an 11–1 record.

The Buckeyes responded. They reeled off 10 wins in a row to win the Big Ten East division. But they lost starting quarterback J. T. Barrett to a broken ankle in the regular-season finale against Michigan. Untested sophomore Cardale Jones had to take over

RUNNING UP THE SCORE

In the 2014 Big Ten Championship Game, Ohio State had the game won by halftime. The Buckeyes led the Wisconsin Badgers 38–0 and pushed that lead to 45–0 entering the fourth quarter. But Urban Meyer chose to leave his starters in the game rather than give some backups the chance to play. Ohio State wasn't assured of a spot in the CFP. Meyer knew he had to beat Wisconsin by as much as possible to show how good the Buckeyes were.

And the Virginia Tech loss still loomed large. The Buckeyes weren't sure if they had done enough to earn one of four spots in the brand new College Football Playoff (CFP). They knew they'd have to use the Big Ten Championship Game to send a message that they were CFP-worthy.

It was a historic rout. Ohio State beat Wisconsin 59–0. It was the Badgers' worst loss since 1979. Jones didn't have to win the game on his own. He just had to be efficient, which he was, completing 12 of 17 passes. The next day, the Buckeyes found out they had made the playoff field.

As the No. 4 seed in the CFP, they had to face the nation's No. 1 team, the Alabama Crimson Tide, in the national semifinals. The game was played in Alabama's back yard, at the Sugar Bowl in New Orleans. And at first, the Tide looked every bit like the dominant team. A Jones interception in the second quarter set up an Alabama touchdown that made the score 21–6.

But once again, the Buckeyes didn't have to rely on Jones to win it for them. They had All-Big Ten running back Ezekiel Elliott. He scored a touchdown on the next drive to pull Ohio State closer.

Cardale Jones handled himself well in relief of J. T. Barrett.

That was the first of four straight touchdowns for the Buckeyes as they surged to a 34–21 lead.

Alabama scored to cut the deficit to six points. But late in the fourth quarter, Elliott came up with the play of the game, an 85-yard touchdown run. The Buckeyes won 42–35. Elliott was named the Sugar Bowl Most Valuable Player (MVP).

✘ Oregon had no answer for Ezekiel Elliott (15) and the Buckeyes offense.

The victory meant Ohio State would play for a national title for the first time in seven years. The Buckeyes' opponent was the Oregon Ducks. Just one more win and their comeback from the Virginia Tech upset would be complete.

Oregon went up 7–0 early, and Ohio State gained just 17 yards on its first drive. But two possessions later, Elliott burst free for a 33-yard touchdown to tie the game. The Buckeyes defense started to clamp down, too.

Jones followed Elliot's touchdown with a 1-yard scoring strike to Nick Vannett late in the first quarter. That put Ohio State on top 14–7. The Buckeyes doubled their lead late in the first half on a 1-yard touchdown run by Jones. However, Oregon had enough time to kick a field goal, making it 21–10 at halftime.

The Ducks were about to make it even more interesting. Jones threw an interception on the Buckeyes' first drive of the second half, and Oregon took advantage. A touchdown pulled the Ducks to within 21–17. On the next Ohio State possession, Jones turned it over again, this time on a fumble. Oregon drove down to kick a field goal, making it a 21–20 game.

A national title was in danger of slipping away. It was time for Elliott to take over. He dominated the rest of the game. Ohio State drove 75 yards, and Elliott finished it off with a 9-yard touchdown run.

The Buckeyes defense then stopped the Ducks, and the offense went on another long drive. Elliott again finished it off with a touchdown. Finally, with time winding down, Elliott put the game away. His fourth touchdown of the game put Ohio State up 42–20. They ran out the clock to clinch an eighth national title.

Elliott was named the game's offensive MVP. For Meyer, it was especially satisfying as he was an Ohio native and Buckeyes fan growing up. Meyer knew the importance of Ohio State football to the people of the Buckeye State. To the fans, having Ohio State back on top as national champion was exactly where it belonged.

CHAPTER 2

BIRTH OF A PROGRAM

It was 1873. The Civil War had ended just eight years earlier. And a new school with only about 24 students opened in the heart of Ohio. It was called the Ohio Agricultural and Mechanical College. In 1878 it was renamed The Ohio State University.

An early variation of football was becoming popular on college campuses throughout the Midwest. It did not take long for students at Ohio State to embrace the sport. On May 3, 1890, an estimated 700 fans witnessed the Buckeyes' first game. The new team defeated Ohio Wesleyan 20–14 in its first game.

Over the years, Ohio State has established itself as one of the most successful college football programs in the nation. But the winning tradition did not start right away. The team lost its other three games in that first year. In fact, it managed just two winning seasons through 1898.

Ohio State fielded its first football team in 1890. The team beat Ohio Wesleyan in its first game.

OHIO STADIUM

Star quarterback Chic Harley created excitement and thousands of new Buckeyes fans. Many believe his influence motivated the school to build a new stadium. Ohio Stadium opened in 1922. It remains the Buckeyes' home. The stadium cost $1.3 million to build. It initially housed 66,000 fans. But the official dedication of what some called "The House That Harley Built" was not a happy one for the Buckeyes. They lost that day to archrival Michigan 19–0.

One defeat hurt more than any other. The Buckeyes faced the Michigan Wolverines for the first time in 1897. Ohio State came into the game with a 1–1 record. The Buckeyes figured they could beat the neighboring team from the north. Instead, they left with a 34–0 loss. And they did not win another game all year. That team's 1–7–1 record remained the worst in Ohio State history through 2019. Coach Dave Edwards was fired after that season.

Few could have anticipated the fierce rivalry that would develop between Ohio State and Michigan. The competition intensified when the Buckeyes got stronger. They began to win consistently around the turn of the century. Under new coach John Eckstrom, they lost just one game from 1899 to 1900. Coaches continued to come and go, but the Buckeyes continued to win. They captured the Ohio Athletic Conference title in 1906 and 1912.

Ohio State moved to the Western Conference in 1913. It was renamed the Big Ten four years later. Ohio State clinched its first conference championship in 1916 with a 23–3 win over Northwestern. The game was tied at 3–3 in the fourth quarter.

Ohio State star quarterback Chic Harley, *right,* stands with Illinois star running back Red Grange.

Then quarterback Chic Harley raced 63 yards for a touchdown. Ohio State ran away with the title after that.

Harley was the Buckeyes' biggest star of that era. One writer from the *Ohio State Journal* newspaper said watching Harley "was kind of a cross between music and cannon fire, and it brought your heart up under your ears."

Ohio State lost just one game with Harley at quarterback. The Buckeyes took home another Big Ten championship in 1917. By that

PAUL BROWN

Ohio State seemed to have its head coach for years to come when it hired 32-year-old Paul Brown in 1941. He had led nearby Massillon Washington High School to five straight state championships. Brown led the Buckeyes to an 18–8–1 record in three seasons. But then he joined the US Navy. Most assumed he would return to coach the team after World War II. However, he was lured away by the new Cleveland team in the All-America Football Conference and, later, the National Football League (NFL). Brown blossomed into one of the most innovative coaches in professional football history.

time, the football program had finally gained stability. John Wilce had taken over as coach in 1913. Until then, no head coach had remained with the team for more than five seasons. Wilce stayed 16 years, finally leaving in 1928. The Buckeyes suffered just three losing seasons under Wilce.

But there was still one problem: they usually lost to Michigan. Heading into the 1934 season, the Wolverines owned a 22–6–2 record against Ohio State. Michigan was also coming off of four straight Big Ten titles.

That year's showdown turned the tables on the rivalry, though. The Buckeyes held Michigan to just 40 total yards in a 34–0 victory. Ohio State went on to hold Michigan scoreless in each of the next three years. The 38–0 win in 1935 secured Ohio State's first Big Ten championship in 15 years.

Ohio State coach Paul Brown diagrams a play for his team in 1941.

The United States entered World War II in 1941. Many young men went to Europe or the Pacific to fight. Some colleges suspended football during the war. Others played freshmen who were too young to be drafted into the army. Fans turned to football as one way to take their minds off the war.

The 1944 Buckeyes provided a great distraction. The team had 31 freshmen among its 43 players. Even so, it entered the game against Michigan undefeated. Michigan, meanwhile, had lost only one game.

Senior quarterback Les Horvath led the Buckeyes. He would go on to win the Heisman Trophy that season as college football's

× Ohio State tailback Vic Janowicz runs for a touchdown against Iowa in 1950. He also starred as a defensive back.

best player. Ohio State trailed 14–12 late in the fourth quarter. But Horvath scored the go-ahead touchdown with three minutes remaining. Then teammate Dick Flanagan intercepted a Michigan pass to seal the victory—and the Big Ten title.

MORE ABOUT LES

Les Horvath did not look like a football star. He was just 5-foot-10 and 173 pounds. But his childhood friend and Ohio State teammate Bob Brugge explained that Horvath had other attributes that made him a Heisman Trophy winner. Brugge wrote, "He was the smartest guy playing football. He was a great tactician who could outthink the opponent."

Horvath spent three years as a halfback for the Los Angeles Rams and the Cleveland Browns before retiring. But he had a backup plan. He had gone to dental school at Ohio State and became a successful dentist.

Vic Janowicz emerged as Ohio State's next star player. Janowicz starred as both a defensive back and a tailback. Ohio State faced California in the Rose Bowl following the 1949 season. The Rose Bowl still hosts the Big Ten champion after most seasons. Janowicz intercepted two passes and returned one for a touchdown in the win.

Janowicz went on to lead the Big Ten in total offense the next season. He also matched Horvath by winning the Heisman Trophy.

Ohio State had featured several great players to that point. However, it was a coach who would cement the program's status as a national power.

CHAPTER 3

THREE YARDS AND A CLOUD OF DUST

In 1951 a Columbus, Ohio, newspaper polled fans on who they thought should be the Buckeyes' next coach. The result was clear: Paul Brown. He had guided the team from 1941 to 1943. Some fans were already campaigning to bring him back. However, a return to Columbus was unlikely. At the time, Brown was coaching the NFL champion Cleveland Browns.

Some readers made light of the newspaper poll. They jokingly suggested names such as movie dog Lassie, actress Lana Turner, and president Harry Truman. Beneath all of those names in the voting, though, was a little-known college coach from Miami University in Ohio. His name was Woody Hayes.

Hayes wanted badly to coach Ohio State. He impressed the hiring committee with his knowledge of the game during a three-hour interview. And soon he had landed his dream job.

Ohio State hired little-known Woody Hayes as head football coach in 1951.

Running back Howard Cassady was a great fit for coach Woody Hayes's "three yards and a cloud of dust" offense.

Hayes was known for his fiery temper. He required discipline from his players. He also ran what some people considered to be a boring offense. It featured a powerful running attack, and the Buckeyes rarely threw the ball. This approach came to be referred to as "three yards and a cloud of dust."

This philosophy would later prove to be very effective. But that was not the case early on. Hayes's teams combined for a 16–9–2 record in his first three seasons. Some people called for Hayes to be fired. Even his players rebelled early on. Once, during his first season, the players locked Hayes out of the locker room. But Hayes made his players stick to his plan without question.

It finally began to pay off in 1954. Junior running back Howard Cassady emerged as a star that year. Cassady and senior quarterback Dave Leggett ran Hayes's offense to perfection. The Buckeyes were 8–0 and ranked number one in the nation when they met Michigan in the final regular-season game. A 21–7 win sent Ohio State to the Rose Bowl to play the University of Southern California (USC) Trojans.

And the Buckeyes dominated. They ran the ball 69 times for 305 yards. The weather that day resembled a monsoon. Yet the Buckeyes didn't lose a fumble. Leggett ran for one touchdown and threw a rare pass for another. Cassady rushed for a team-high 92 yards in the 20–7 victory.

Hayes was thrilled. He stood on a bench in the locker room and praised his players. "You're the number-one team!" he said. Hayes, now a national

FULL OF FULLBACKS

Buckeyes coach Woody Hayes used a power running game to wear down defenses. He recruited strong fullbacks to pound away for yardage. When one great fullback graduated, another one filled his spot. Such was the case in the late 1960s. Jim Otis combined for more than 2,000 rushing yards and 32 touchdowns in 1968 and 1969. When Otis left to play in the NFL, John Brockington took over at fullback. He ran for 1,142 yards and 17 touchdowns in 1970.

TERRIFIC TATUM

Of all the great defensive players during the Woody Hayes era, safety Jack Tatum stood out. He was known for his tight coverage and hard tackles. Perhaps his best game was as a sophomore in 1968. Tatum shut down super Purdue running back Leroy Keyes by following him all over the field. The victory over top-ranked Purdue gave the Buckeyes momentum, and they rode all the way to the national championship.

"To this day, that was as good a defensive game as I've ever seen somebody play," Ohio State football historian Jack Park said. "And he was about as good as it gets. We've had a lot of great defensive players play at Ohio State, but I think if you had to pick one, it would be Jack Tatum." Tatum went on to star with the NFL's Oakland Raiders.

championship winner, was becoming known as one of the top coaches in college football.

That reputation grew stronger over the years. The Buckeyes suffered just two losing seasons during Hayes's 28 years at Ohio State. But fans had become antsy by 1968. Ohio State had not won a Big Ten championship in seven years. That was the longest drought since the 1930s.

But that drought ended in 1968. Hayes again built his team around a strong group of underclassmen. Bruising fullback Jim Otis led the offense. Jim Stillwagon led a strong group of linebackers on defense. And by that time, Hayes had also become open to allowing quarterback Rex Kern to throw the ball more often.

Safety Jack Tatum was known for his hard tackles while playing for Ohio State from 1968 to 1970.

The Buckeyes began the season ranked No. 11 in the country. They climbed to number two after shutting out top-ranked Purdue 13–0 in their third game. The Buckeyes rolled after that. They closed out the regular season with a 50–14 thumping over fourth-ranked Michigan. That win finally gave Ohio State the top ranking. USC was

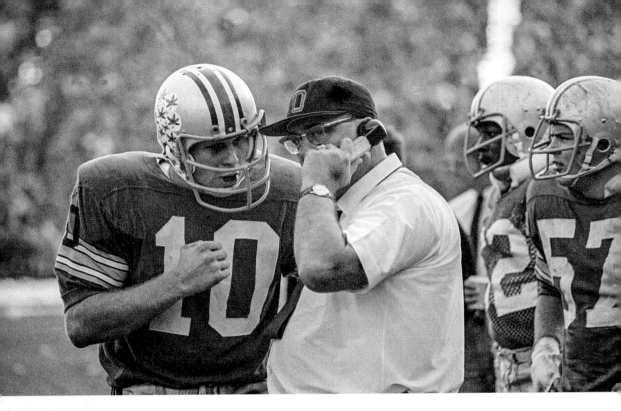

✗ Ohio State quarterback Rex Kern (10) discusses strategy with coach Woody Hayes during a 50–14 blowout of Michigan in 1968.

ranked number two. They met in the Rose Bowl to determine the national champion.

Ohio State's defense had been average that season. It faced a huge challenge in USC superstar running back O. J. Simpson. The Buckeyes would also have to play in front of 102,000 fans, many of whom were cheering for the hometown Trojans.

The Buckeyes fell behind 10–0 in the second quarter. Simpson was running wild with 137 yards in the first half alone. But Ohio State roared back to tie the game at halftime. Kern tossed two touchdown passes. That helped the Buckeyes secure the 27–16 victory. Otis finished with 101 rushing yards. Meanwhile, the defense held Simpson to just 34 yards in the second half. The Buckeyes had earned their first national title in 14 years.

After the game, Simpson visited the Ohio State locker room. "You're the best ball team in the country, and don't let anybody tell you that you aren't," he told the Buckeyes.

The future looked bright for Ohio State. Eleven of the team's 22 starters from the 1968 championship team were back the next year as juniors. They kept rolling in 1969. Ohio State averaged 46 points per game on its way to an 8–0 record. It won every game during that stretch by at least 27 points. All that stood in the way of another Rose Bowl appearance was twelfth-ranked Michigan.

Most assumed the top-ranked Buckeyes would cruise past the Wolverines. But Michigan's first-year head coach, Bo Schembechler, had other ideas. He had played for Hayes at Miami and later served as his assistant coach at Ohio State. Schembechler wanted to defeat his former boss. And that is just what he did. A sellout crowd of 103,000 fans showed up for the game in Ann Arbor, Michigan. The Wolverines came out with a 24–12 victory. It is still considered one of the greatest upsets in college football history. Hayes later expressed shock that Michigan had defeated what he considered his best-ever team.

Hayes and his Buckeyes came back to beat Michigan the next year. Ohio State continued to dominate the Big Ten well into the 1970s. But Hayes's legendary temper got the best of him one night in 1978. And Ohio State football would never be the same.

CHAPTER 4

CHANGES

The 1970s were a great era for Ohio State football. Between 1970 and 1977, Ohio State captured or shared the Big Ten title in all but one season. In addition, halfback Archie Griffin won the Heisman trophy in 1974 and 1975. Through 2019 he remained the only player to win the award twice. The Buckeyes went a combined 31–3–1 from 1973 to 1975.

But that overwhelming success didn't carry over to their rivalry with Michigan. From 1971 to 1978, the Wolverines beat the Buckeyes four times and tied them once. The tie in 1973 ended the Buckeyes' shot at a national title. The "three yards and a cloud of dust" offense managed just nine total points in falling to Michigan in 1976, 1977, and 1978.

The Buckeyes were invited to the Gator Bowl in 1978. The Gator Bowl is not as prestigious as the bowl games Ohio State had been used to playing. That year's game soon became notable, but not for anything Ohio State achieved on the field.

Ohio State halfback Archie Griffin won the Heisman Trophy in 1974 and 1975.

THE GREAT GRIFFIN

Before 1972 college freshmen were not allowed to play on varsity sports teams. When the rule changed, Ohio State freshman running back Archie Griffin was ready. He rushed for 867 yards in 1972. Then he exploded for 1,577 yards as a sophomore. He posted career bests with 1,695 yards and 12 touchdowns the following year. He completed his college career by rushing for 1,450 yards as a senior. Through 2019 Griffin remains the only player to win two Heisman Trophies. He left Ohio State as the leading rusher in college football history with 5,589 yards.

Some people said Griffin was not quick or fast enough to star in the NFL. They were mostly right. Griffin played seven seasons with the Cincinnati Bengals but never rushed for more than 700 yards in any of them. Brother Ray Griffin, who followed Archie to Ohio State as a defensive back, also played for the Bengals in the 1970s and 1980s.

The Buckeyes trailed Clemson 17–15 with two minutes remaining. They had the ball and were driving. However, the comeback attempt ended when Clemson defensive lineman Charlie Bauman intercepted a pass. The defeat was too much for Hayes to handle. As Bauman ran out of bounds on the Ohio State sideline, Hayes punched him under his chin and took two more swings at him. Hayes then slugged one of his own players who was trying to restrain him.

The Woody Hayes era at Ohio State was over. He refused to resign so Ohio State fired him. University president Harold Enarson

✕ Woody Hayes lashes out at an Ohio State player trying to restrain him at the end of the 1978 Gator Bowl.

explained the decision, saying, "There's not a university or athletic conference in the country that would permit a coach to physically assault a college athlete."

Iowa State coach Earle Bruce was hired to replace Hayes. Bruce made a grand entrance. Ohio State went unbeaten in his first Big Ten season. That included a dramatic 18–15 victory over Michigan. Bruce guided the Buckeyes to the number-one ranking in the country and the doorstep of a national championship. The team then built

Before the College Football Playoff and the Bowl Championship Series (BCS) that preceded it, there was no national championship game. Voters in polls such as the Associated Press (AP) Poll cast their ballots at the end of the year with who they thought was the best team. Because there were numerous polls, sometimes more than one team claimed the national title. Ohio State claims eight national titles: in 1942, 1954, 1957, 1961, 1968, 1970, 2002, and 2014. But in some of these years, Ohio State was picked in just a few polls. In 1961, for example, 11–0 Alabama was the choice of most polls, including AP. The Buckeyes at 8–0–1 were picked by lesser polls such as the Football Writers Association of America.

a 16–10 lead over USC in the Rose Bowl. However, the Trojans scored the winning touchdown with less than two minutes remaining.

It was the closest Bruce would get to a national title as Ohio State's coach. The Buckeyes lost at least three games in each of the next eight years. Bruce recruited many of the best players in the nation. But that did not always bring victories. The Buckeyes stumbled at some point every season, often losing to weaker opponents.

In 1987 the Buckeyes suffered their first loss to lowly Indiana since 1951. Losses to Michigan State, Wisconsin, and Iowa followed. The school announced that it would fire Bruce after the annual showdown against Michigan. Bruce went out on a high note. He coached his team to a tough 23–20 victory on the road over the Wolverines. His players carried him off the field after the game.

Arizona State head coach John Cooper was hired to replace Bruce. Like Bruce, Cooper had a lot of success recruiting. But he had even less success than Bruce when it came to actually winning, especially at first. The Buckeyes finished 4–6–1 during Cooper's first season, in 1988. It was their first losing record in 22 years.

Cooper's teams lost 21 games over his first five seasons. More disturbing than that, though, was his record against Michigan. Cooper went winless in his first six meetings against what Ohio State fans referred to mockingly as "that school up north."

But Cooper eventually got the Buckeyes turned in the right direction. Star running back Eddie George won the Heisman Trophy in 1995. Meanwhile, the team went unbeaten until the Michigan games in 1993, 1995, and 1996. Each time, a win over Michigan would have sent Ohio State into a bowl game with a chance to win the national title. Yet Ohio State fell to Michigan all three times.

The trend continued in 1998. The Buckeyes outscored their first eight opponents 306–72. They were the top-ranked team in the nation. The Michigan State Spartans did not appear to be much of a threat in the next game. And the Buckeyes led the Spartans 24–9 early in the third quarter. But Ohio State did not score another point. Michigan State roared back for a 28–24 victory in front of 93,000 stunned fans at Ohio Stadium. Yet another dream season had turned into a nightmare.

"All losses hurt, but this one especially," said Buckeyes senior quarterback Joe Germaine. "It was very quiet in the

Ohio State linebacker Chris Spielman won the 1987 Lombardi Award as the nation's top lineman or linebacker.

locker room [after the loss], and it should be. We had some high expectations for this team."

Each season under Cooper seemed to be the same story. Ohio State began with high expectations. But then it would lose an unexpected game and fall short of a national title. Many fans called for Cooper to be fired in 1998. However, he remained for two more seasons. After losing six games in 1999 and four more in 2000, though, those fans got their wish.

Cooper left Ohio State with a 2–10–1 record against Michigan. And his teams were just 3–8 in bowl games. No Ohio State coach could survive with such a terrible mark against the Wolverines and in the postseason. Cooper was soon replaced by a man who could turn that around. The Jim Tressel era was about to begin.

TERRIFIC TACKLER

Perhaps the most important task for any linebacker is to make tackles all over the field. That ability is what made Chris Spielman one of best linebackers in football. Spielman was known for his passion as a player. He won the 1987 Lombardi Award. It is presented to the top lineman in college football. He continued to shine as a linebacker for the NFL's Detroit Lions. Spielman recorded 153 tackles as a rookie. He added 100 or more in eight of the next nine seasons before injuries cut his career short.

CHAPTER 5

A NEW CHAMPIONSHIP ERA

Ohio State hired Jim Tressel from Youngstown State in 2001. The jump from Youngstown to Ohio State was big. But Tressel had grown up in Ohio, and he knew what was important to Buckeyes fans. Tressel spoke to Ohio State fans at one of the school's men's basketball games after he was hired. He stressed how important it would be to beat Michigan.

Tressel backed up his talk. The Buckeyes beat the Wolverines in 2001 and 2002. Those were their first back-to-back victories over "that school up north" in 20 years.

The team needed a fantastic finish to beat Michigan in the last regular-season game of 2002. It all came down to one final play. The Buckeyes had a lot riding on that play. A win would give them a perfect 13–0 season and a shot at the national championship.

Ohio State Coach Jim Tressel helped lead the Buckeyes back to the mountaintop.

Michigan quarterback John Navarre fired a pass toward the end zone. But Ohio State defensive back Will Allen made sure it didn't reach its intended target. He intercepted the ball and sealed the victory. The crowd poured onto the field to celebrate with the team.

But Ohio State and its second-year head coach went beyond merely winning a rivalry game that season. The BCS was created in 1998 to pit the nation's eight best teams against each other in four bowl games. One of the four bowls served as the national championship game. The Fiesta Bowl was the championship game after the 2002 season. The Buckeyes and the Miami Hurricanes were selected to participate.

The game was a thriller that was tied 17–17 going into overtime. The Hurricanes scored first. Ohio State then drove to the Miami 5-yard line before throwing an incomplete pass on fourth down. Miami players and fans rushed onto the field to celebrate. Fireworks lit up the night sky. But the jubilation was premature. Miami was called for pass interference.

The Buckeyes were still alive. On their second chance, quarterback Craig Krenzel scored on a 1-yard plunge to force a second overtime. This time Ohio State started with the ball. The Buckeyes took a 31–24 lead on a touchdown run by talented freshman running back Maurice Clarett. The Hurricanes responded. They drove to the Ohio State 2-yard line. But the Buckeyes' defense stopped them on the next three plays. Now they just needed to do it one last time.

✗ Maurice Clarett (13) tunnels his way into the end zone in the second overtime against Miami.

The Buckeyes called for a blitz. Senior linebacker Cie Grant barreled across the line. Just as Miami quarterback Ken Dorsey cocked his arm to throw, Grant grabbed his jersey. The ball fluttered into the air and fell harmlessly to the turf. A brilliant goal-line stand had secured the Buckeyes' first national championship in 34 years.

✗ Ohio State quarterback Troy Smith calls a play during a 2006 game. He won that year's Heisman Trophy.

The Buckeyes had another chance for a national title in 2006. Senior quarterback and Heisman Trophy winner Troy Smith led the way. An elite defense helped the Buckeyes reach the BCS National Championship Game against Florida. Ohio State came into the game ranked number one, with Florida ranked number two. The Buckeyes got off to a strong start. Speedy wide receiver Ted Ginn ran the opening kickoff back for a touchdown. However, Ginn injured his foot while celebrating the score. He played just one series before missing the rest of the game. And the Gators dominated from there. They cruised to a 41–14 victory.

Ohio State went 11–1 in the 2007 regular season. Sophomore running back Chris "Beanie" Wells rushed for 1,609 yards. Three-time All-America linebacker James Laurinaitis led an outstanding defense. The Buckeyes made it back to the BCS Championship Game. This time they faced Louisiana State (LSU) for the national title. But Ohio State again fell flat. The team's strong defense was shredded for 21 points in the second quarter alone. The Buckeyes made mistake after mistake. LSU emerged with a 38–24 victory.

The future looked bright for more national championships and more victories over Michigan. Tressel signed a new contract in March 2010 that would have kept him in Columbus through 2014. But he resigned in scandal before the 2011 season.

QUALITY QUARTERBACK

When discussing the greatest Ohio State quarterbacks of all time, Troy Smith's name is sure to come up. Smith was not even supposed to play at that position as a sophomore. But he got the nod when starter Justin Zwick got hurt in 2004. Smith took the job and ran with it. He improved every year with the Buckeyes.

Smith completed more than 64 percent of his passes during his last two seasons at Ohio State. During that time, Smith threw 46 touchdown passes and just 10 interceptions. He peaked as a senior in 2006 with 30 touchdowns and six interceptions. For his efforts, Smith won the Heisman Trophy that year.

Ohio State quarterback Justin Fields takes off running against Clemson in the 2019 Fiesta Bowl.

About a month after signing his extension, Tressel received an email claiming that Ohio State players had sold memorabilia, such as old uniforms and championship rings. That is against the rules in college sports. Tressel replied that he would investigate. However, he violated the rules by failing to report the information to school officials. Tressel resigned on May 30, 2011. Ohio State was also forced to vacate all 12 of its victories and its Big Ten title from 2010.

Replacement coach Luke Fickell struggled to maintain greatness on the field. The 2011 Buckeyes finished the regular season with a 6–6 record. One of those losses was to Michigan. It was the Buckeyes' first loss to the Wolverines since 2003.

Ohio State fans knew who they wanted as their next coach. Urban Meyer had led Florida to two national championships.

Included was the triumph over Ohio State following the 2006 season. Meyer had also grown up in Ohio a Buckeyes fan. Ohio State hired Meyer to coach the team in 2012.

The Meyer era started off smoothly. The 2012 Buckeyes went 12–0, but due to the Tressel incident the team was banned from playing in the postseason. But Ohio State was dominant throughout the Meyer era, losing just nine games in his seven seasons. The team won at least a share of the Big Ten's East Division every year. The highlight was the 2014 national title.

The Meyer era wasn't all perfect, though. Meyer was suspended for three games at the start of the 2018 season for failing to properly handle a report of assault against one of his assistant coaches. Then, about a month before the team played in the Rose Bowl in January 2019, Meyer announced he was retiring from coaching. He cited the suspension and some ongoing health concerns as his reasons.

Assistant Ryan Day took over the program while Meyer was suspended. He later was chosen to succeed Meyer full-time as well. Day inherited a program in the middle of one of the greatest eras in its proud history. He had a tough job to do to maintain that high standard of success. In his first year, at least, he did it. Ohio State went undefeated in the regular season and won the Big Ten Championship Game. The Buckeyes advanced to the national semifinals, where they lost a heartbreaker to Clemson in the Fiesta Bowl. Ohio State fans were excited to see what the future had in store for Day and his team.

TIMELINE

1890 — Ohio State beats Ohio Wesleyan 20–14 on May 3 in its first football game.

1897 — The Ohio State–Michigan rivalry kicks off on October 16 with a 34–0 Wolverines victory.

1913 — The Buckeyes move to the Western Conference, which is later renamed the Big Ten Conference.

1916 — Sophomore quarterback Chic Harley leads the Buckeyes to a 23–3 win over Northwestern and their first Western Conference title on November 25.

1922 — Ohio Stadium is dedicated with a capacity of 65,000 on October 21 as Michigan defeats Ohio State 19–0.

1942 — Paul Brown coaches the Buckeyes to their first national championship with a 9–1 record.

1951 — Ohio State hires Woody Hayes as its new head football coach on February 18.

1955 — Having wrapped up their second national title, the Buckeyes defeat USC 20–7 in the Rose Bowl on January 1 to finish the season 10–0.

1969 — Ohio State tops USC 27–16 in the Rose Bowl on New Year's Day to clinch an unbeaten season and the national championship.

1975 — Running back Archie Griffin becomes the only player in college football history through 2019 to win the Heisman Trophy twice.

Hayes punches Clemson player Charlie Bauman on December 29 and is quickly fired.

✕

1978

Hopes for a national title in Earle Bruce's first season are dashed by a 17–16 loss to USC in the Rose Bowl on January 1.

✕

1980

Jim Tressel coaches the Buckeyes to their first national championship in 34 years with a thrilling 31–24 win in double overtime against Miami on January 3.

✕

2003

The Buckeyes begin a stretch in which they win or share the next six Big Ten championships.

✕

2005

Senior quarterback Troy Smith becomes the sixth Ohio State player to win the Heisman Trophy.

✕

2006

Florida upsets Ohio State 41–14 in the BCS National Championship Game on January 8.

✕

2007

The Buckeyes fall for the second straight year in the BCS title game in a 38–24 loss to LSU on January 7.

✕

2008

Tressel resigns as head coach on May 30. Ohio native and former Florida coach Urban Meyer is hired as coach on November 28.

✕

2011

The Buckeyes beat Oregon 42–20 on January 12 to clinch the program's eighth national championship.

✕

2015

Citing health concerns and the effects of a suspension, Meyer retires from coaching following the Buckeyes' Rose Bowl win on January 1.

✕

2019

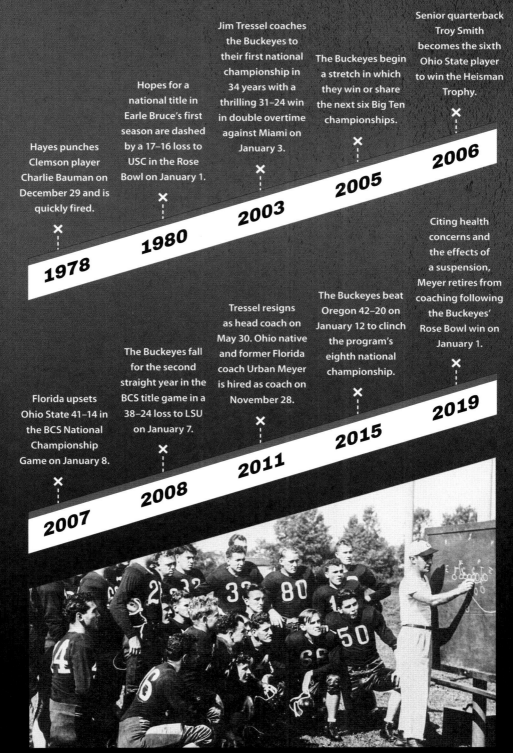

43

QUICK STATS

PROGRAM INFO

Ohio State University Buckeyes
(1890–)

NATIONAL CHAMPIONSHIPS

1942, 1954*, 1957*, 1961*, 1968,
1970*, 2002, 2014

OTHER ACHIEVEMENTS

Conference championships: 40
Division titles: 8
Bowl record: 25–26

KEY COACHES

John Cooper (1988–2000)
111–43–4, 3–8 (bowl games)
Woody Hayes (1951–78)
205–61–10, 5–6 (bowl games)
Urban Meyer (2012–18)
83–9, 5–2 (bowl games)
Jim Tressel (2001–10)
106–22, 6–4 (bowl games)

KEY PLAYERS

Joey Bosa (DL, 2013–15)
Cris Carter (WR, 1984–86)
Howard Cassady (RB, 1952–55)**
Ezekiel Elliott (RB, 2013–15)
Eddie George (RB, 1992–95)**
Archie Griffin (RB, 1972–75)**
Chic Harley (HB, 1916–17, 1919)
Les Horvath (QB, 1940–42, 1944)**
Vic Janowicz (RB-DB, 1949–51)**
James Laurinaitis (LB, 2005–08)
Orlando Pace (OT, 1994–96)
Troy Smith (QB, 2003–06)**
Chris Spielman (LB, 1984–87)
Jim Stillwagon (LB, 1968–70)
Jack Tatum (DB, 1968–70)

HOME STADIUM

Ohio Stadium (1922–)

*Denotes shared title
**Heisman Trophy winner
All statistics through 2019 season

QUOTES AND ANECDOTES

It is rare for a university to nickname its sports teams after a tree, but Ohio State teams are called the Buckeyes after buckeye trees, which are common in the state. In fact, Ohio is known as "The Buckeye State."

"The tradition we have gets in your blood and remains there. . . . It's unlike any other place in the world—it's such a special place."

—Two-time Heisman Trophy winner Archie Griffin on the Ohio State tradition

One of the most beloved college football traditions is commentator Lee Corso donning the headgear of the mascot of the team he picks to win the big game of the day on ESPN's *College GameDay*. The tradition started at Ohio State. The show was broadcasting from Columbus on October 5, 1996. Third-ranked Ohio State was playing No. 4 Penn State later that day. To add a little extra excitement to his pick, Corso stashed the head of Ohio State mascot Brutus Buckeye under the desk. When he picked the Buckeyes, Corso donned Brutus's head and the crowd went wild. Corso has kept up the tradition every week since.

One Buckeye who could not display his talent under Woody Hayes was wide receiver Paul Warfield. Hayes simply did not allow his quarterbacks to throw the ball often, particularly during Warfield's playing days in the early 1960s. Therefore, Warfield caught just 39 passes in three seasons, and just 17 in his first two. But he later blossomed to become a Hall of Fame receiver in the NFL with the Cleveland Browns and Miami Dolphins.

INDEX

ABOUT THE AUTHOR

Tony Hunter is a writer from Castle Rock, Colorado. He lives with his daughter and his trusty Rottweiler, Dan.